SPACE FIELD GUIDE

Activities, Doodling, and Fun Facts

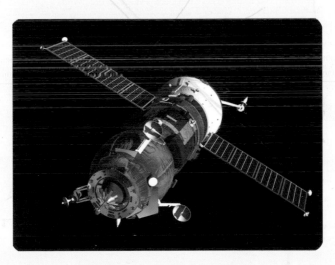

Written by Cynthia Stierle

Silver Dolphin
San Diego, California

Comet Tail Trail

You don't have to go far for a space adventure. Sometimes you can see comets shooting across the night sky right here from Earth. Which of the comets below flew the nearest to Earth? (Answer on page 22.)

hart the Solar System

ur planets are missing from the grid below. Each planet
ould appear once in each column and once in each row.
se the stickers that came with this book to fill in the grid with
e missing planets. (Answer on page 22.)

Back in Orbit

There are eight major planets in our solar system, but they're out of orbit! Use the stickers that came with this book to put all eight planets back in their correct orbits.

Mars

9

2

Venus

3

Earth

4

Mercury

Uranus

Neptune

5

Jupiter

8

Saturn

Telescopic View

The Hubble Space Telescope can look farther into space than any Earth-based telescope. But someone has zoomed in a little too close. Match the close-up pictures below with the full-view pictures on the opposite page. (Answers on page 22.)

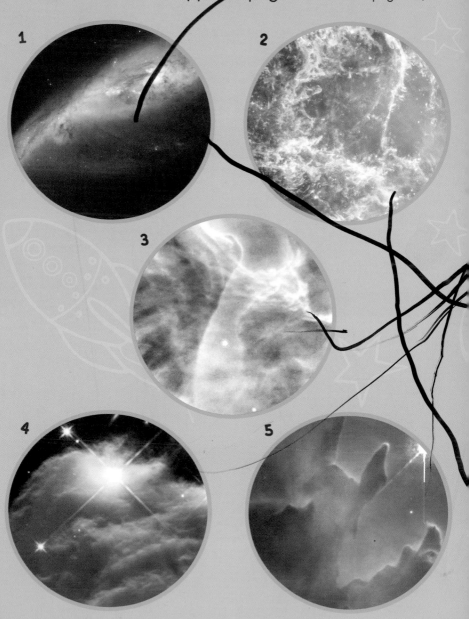

1

2

3

4

5

B

C

E

A 5   B 4.   c 3

D 1   E 2

9

Sightseeing

What could you see when you're exploring space? Look at the pictures below and identify some things you might find. Then in the crossword boxes with the names of those objects. We'v done one for you to help you get started. (Answers on page 22.)

Across

2

4

7

8

Down

1

2

3

5

6

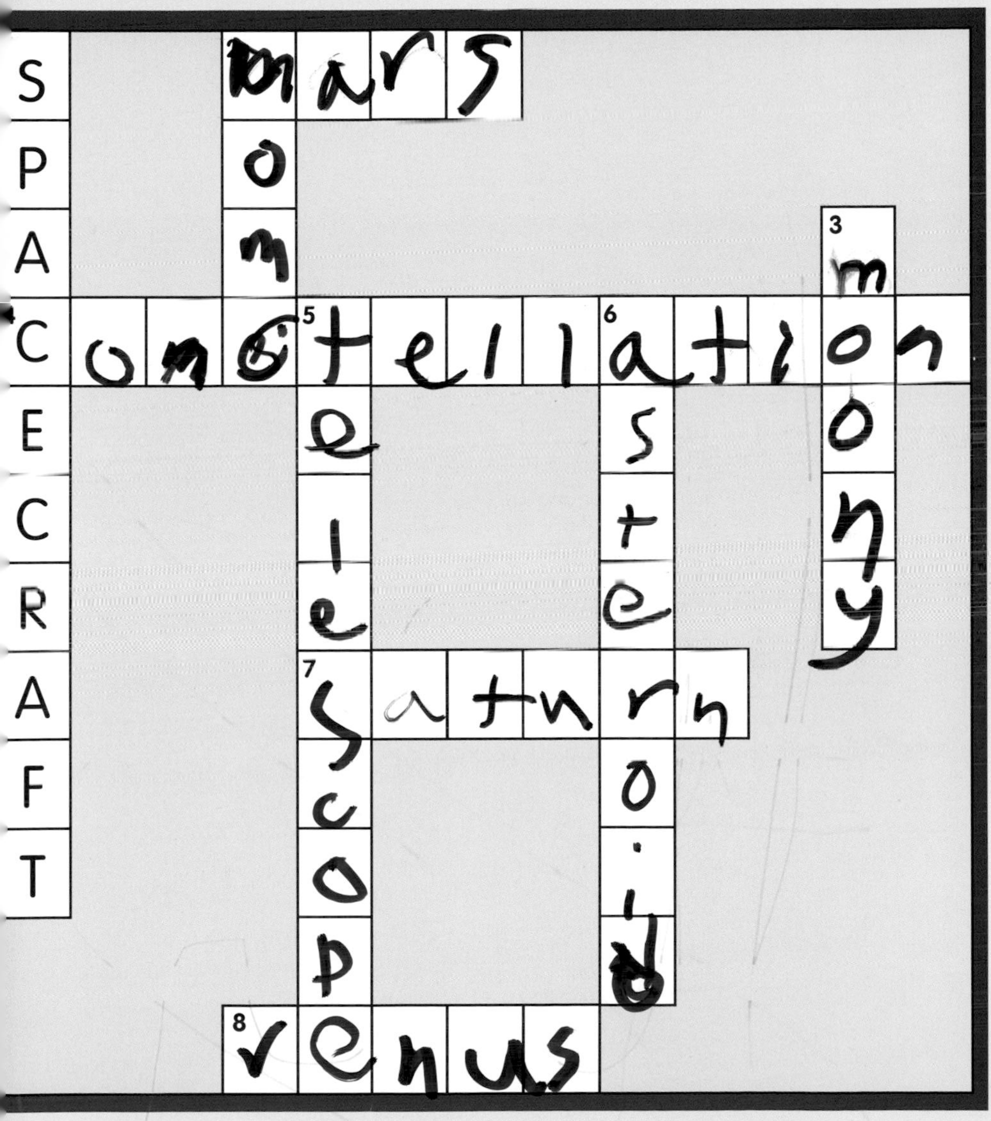

MARS
SPACECRAFT
VENUS

MOON
CONSTELLATION
COMET

TELESCOPE
SATURN
ASTEROID

Look Out!

Guide the spacecraft safely through the space debris.

(Answer on page 22.)

Start

Finish

Back to the Drawing Board: Design a Spacecraft

To explore the outer reaches of space, you will need an amazing vehicle. Draw the spacecraft you would use to travel to the stars.

What's Different?

The robotic craft *Curiosity* is exploring the surface of Mars. Look at the two pictures. There are five differences between them. Can you find them all?

(Answers on page 22.)

What do you see that is different?

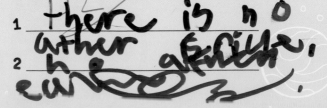

1. there is no other
2. he

3 ___There is no___
atmor eye cudtum
4 _____
5 ___No nitrae___

Star Search

It takes practice to look up at the sky and recognize different constellations. It might be easier to find them hidden in the grid below. The names of the constellations are listed on the opposite page. Look across, down, and diagonally to find them.

(Answers on page 22.)

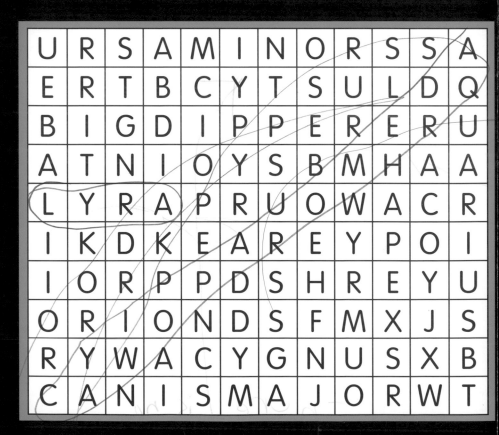

U	R	S	A	M	I	N	O	R	S	S	A
E	R	T	B	C	Y	T	S	U	L	D	Q
B	I	G	D	I	P	P	E	R	E	R	U
A	T	N	I	O	Y	S	B	M	H	A	A
L	Y	R	A	P	R	U	O	W	A	C	R
I	K	D	K	E	A	R	E	Y	P	O	I
I	O	R	P	P	D	S	H	R	E	Y	U
O	R	I	O	N	D	S	F	M	X	J	S
R	Y	W	A	C	Y	G	N	U	S	X	B
C	A	N	I	S	M	A	J	O	R	W	T

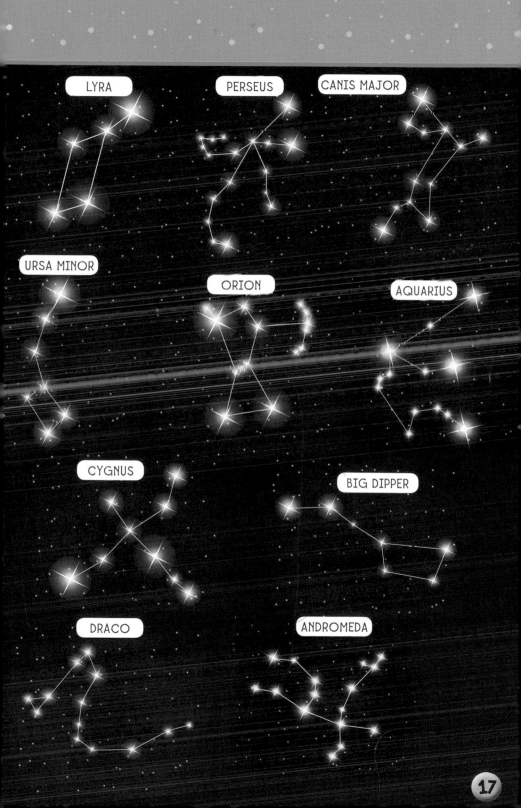

You Name It

Imagine you are living in ancient times and are looking at the stars. Draw your own starry pattern in the telescope lens frame below. Then connect the stars to make a picture and a brand-new constellation.

What do you call it?

_____

Which planet receives the Sun's light in a little over eight minutes?

To answer the question above, read each statement below. If a statement is true for one of the planets, write an X in the box below that planet. The planet that remains is the answer to the question! (Answer on page 22.)

1. This planet has no moons.

2. This is the biggest planet.

3. This planet is famous for its rings.

☐ Earth

☑ Jupiter

☐ Saturn

☐ Mercury

For the Space Log

Exploring space is exciting because there's no limit to what you can find. There are as many as 400 billion stars in our galaxy alone. Some of those stars have planets that orbit them, just as Earth orbits the Sun.

Imagine you have discovere a new planet. Draw a picture of it.

No one knows if there are other forms of life in the universe. But the universe is so big, there might be.

Draw a picture of what you think a being on another planet might look like.

Answers

PAGE 4: Comet 3

PAGE 5:

PAGES 8-9: A4, B5, C3, D1, E2

PAGES 10-11:

	S		M	O	O	N		
	P		A					
	A		R				C	
	C	O	N	S	T	E	L	L	A	T	I	O	N
	E		S				A		M
	C		E				S		E
	R		L				T		T
	A		E		S	A	T	U	R	N
	F		C				R		O
	T		O				O		I
			P				I		D
			V	E	N	U	S

PAGE 12:

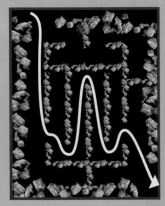

PAGES 14-15:

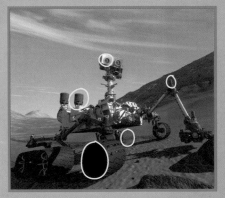

PAGES 16-17:

U	R	S	A	M	I	N	O	R	S	S	A
E	R	T	B	C	Y	T	S	U	L	D	Q
B	I	G	D	I	P	P	E	R	E	R	U
A	T	N	I	O	Y	S	B	M	H	A	A
L	Y	R	A	P	R	U	O	W	A	C	R
I	K	D	K	E	A	R	E	Y	P	O	I
I	O	R	P	P	D	S	H	R	E	Y	U
O	R	I	O	N	D	S	F	M	X	J	S
R	Y	W	A	C	Y	G	N	U	S	X	B
C	A	N	I	S	M	A	J	O	R	W	T

PAGE 19: Earth

22